This book belongs to

_____

...a girl after God's own heart.

A Girl After God's Own Heart

Elizabeth George

HARVEST HOUSE PUBLISHERS
EUGENE, OREGON

Unless otherwise indicated, all Scripture quotations are taken from the Holy Bible, New International Version®, NIV®. Copyright © 1973, 1978, 1984 by Biblica, Inc.™ Used by permission of Zondervan. All rights reserved worldwide.

Verses marked NKJV are taken from the New King James Version. Copyright © 1982 by Thomas Nelson, Inc. Used by permission. All rights reserved.

Verses marked TLB are taken from The Living Bible, Copyright © 1971. Used by permission of Tyndale House Publishers, Inc., Wheaton, IL 60189 USA. All rights reserved.

Cover by Garborg Design Works, Savage, Minnesota

A GIRL AFTER GOD'S OWN HEART
Copyright © 2010 by Elizabeth George
Published by Harvest House Publishers
Eugene, Oregon 97402
www.harvesthousepublishers.com

Library of Congress Cataloging-in-Publication Data
 George, Elizabeth.
 A girl after God's own heart / Elizabeth George.
  p. cm.
 ISBN 978-0-7369-1768-1 (pbk.)
 ISBN 978-0-7369-3754-2 (eBook)
  1. Girls—Religious life—Juvenile literature. 2. Preteens—Religious life—Juvenile literature. 3. Christian life—Biblical teaching—Juvenile literature. I. Title.
 BV4551.3.G46 2010
 248.8'2—dc22

                 2009053824

Printed in the United States of America

    15 16 17 18 19 20 / VP-SK / 23 22 21 20

This book is lovingly dedicated to my granddaughters,
my own "girls" after God's own heart—

Taylor Zaengle
Katie Seitz
Grace Seitz
Lilyanna Seitz

May you enjoy every step of your
many adventures with Jesus!

Delight yourself in the LORD
and he will give you the desires of your heart.

Commit your way to the LORD;
trust in him and he will do this.

—PSALM 37:4 AND 5

Contents

Introduction

A Note Just for You

Hi there!

I'm Elizabeth, and I'm so glad to meet you! And I'm so glad you are holding this book in your hands. I cannot tell you how excited I am that you and I are going to go on a journey together with Jesus! I've also invited a girl named Emma to come along with us. She's a tween girl just like you who loves God and wants to be a girl after His own heart.

As you prepare to make this exciting trip, here's a little list to get you started on your adventure.

Open your book...

...and enjoy it. It's just a book! It's not homework. It's not assigned reading. It's not a chore. No, I wrote this book to be a fun adventure. Everything you need is here—except your favorite pen or pencil. I even put the Bible verses in the book for you. And if you have your own Bible handy, great!

Open your heart...

...to your friends. It will be so neat to go on this adventure with your best girl friends! The more girls you get together, the merrier your adventure will be. And if your mom is your best girl friend, you're lucky. Ask her to go through the book with you.

...and pray. Ask Jesus to help you realize how much He loves you. Also, ask Him to help you understand what it means to be a girl after His own heart.

...and dream! Dream about your future. Dream about all the cool things you want to do, love to do, and hope to do. You are very special, and it never hurts to dream your special dreams. They are a part of the wonderful person you are. I know you'll pick up lots of tips from this book that will help you live out your Number One dream—to be a girl after God's own heart!

Are you ready to let the fun begin? I am! As you read, please remember that every page of this book is covered with my prayers for you. And every word has been written with you in my mind and in my heart. I've had you in my heart as I sit here in my office thinking about you, praying for you, and writing to you. I've also tried hard to imagine you at home—whether it's in a city apartment or a suburban home or a farmhouse out on the plains. And I've tried to picture you in your room and with your family. When I say that I consider you to be a friend without even meeting you in person, I mean it!

Soooo—ready...set...here we go!

In Jesus' great and amazing love,
Your friend and sister-in-Christ,

Elizabeth George

1

My Heart

mma? Emma! Emma Thomas!" Mrs. Jones barked out. It wasn't until Emma's friend Jenny shook her arm that Emma refocused her gaze from looking out the window and realized that everyone in her class was staring at her.

"Could you please repeat the question, Mrs. Jones?" Emma sheepishly asked her history teacher.

Emma had been a complete mess ever since she'd received an invitation to Tiffany's birthday party. That was a week ago, and Emma was still caught up in the thrill of being invited to a party given by the coolest girl in her class. For months Emma had been totally absorbed in breaking into the "cool girl" circle. At last it looked like her hard work was finally paying off. And now that she was about to be "in" with this group of girls, she wanted to focus on how to stay in the "in" circle.

FUN IN GOD'S WORD!

Lots of things in our lives attract our attention and distract us from what's truly important. For Emma it was a birthday invitation that took her mind off her schoolwork—and everything else. She just couldn't stop thinking about that birthday party!

So, what's the problem? What's wrong with a party and having some fun? Well, nothing, of course! But the real issue was the focus of Emma's heart. What she really need-ed was a better understanding of where God wants His girls to focus their hearts.

To help you take a closer look at the heart—*your* heart—let's have some fun with the acrostic below that spells out H-E-A-R-T. I'm guessing you have a favorite pen or pencil, or a favorite color of ink. (Mine is turquoise!) Whatever your favorite is, get it out and keep it handy. An adventure with Jesus and a trip into God's Word are about to begin!

As you read the verses in the following chapters, you may want to mark what you like and learn. And feel free to write all over the margins! Also try to answer the ques-tions, even if only in your mind. And if you don't have a pen handy or you only feel like reading, that's fine! I want reading this book to be fun—not feel like another home-work assignment.

Well, here goes! Whisper a prayer to God, and ask Him to work in your heart.

Have a heart check-up. Wow, was Jesus ever right on when He told the people who wanted to follow Him, "Where your treasure is, there your heart will be also" (Mat-thew 6:21). For Emma, her "treasure"—her heart—was in friends, parties, and the "in" crowd. For other girls, their heart's treasure may be in getting straight A's, winning trophies in gymnastics, or wearing the right clothes.

Now the big question is, where's *your* treasure? Where's *your* focus? Where's *your* heart? A girl after God's own heart wants to be sure her treasure—what she thinks is most valuable and important—is what God says it should be.

As you begin this adventure in loving Jesus and following Him, here's a very important verse that shows you what God wants to be first in your life. It's Acts 13:22—and it's dynamite! In this verse God describes the heart of the man He chose to be king over His people. Here's what He says:

> *I have found David son of Jesse a man after My own heart; he will do everything I want him to do.* What does a person after God's own heart do that sets him or her apart?

_____

_____

My new friend, this is the goal of this book—that you be growing into a *girl* after God's own heart, a girl who follows God and is willing to go on the adventure of doing whatever He wants you to do. Does this sound impossible? Well, it's not. Read on!

Experience God's love. Having a heart for God starts with realizing that God loves you. As much as your parents and grandparents love you, no one loves you more than God. The Bible tells us these things about God's love:

God is love (1 John 4:8). What do you learn about God in this verse?

_____

_____

God so loved the world [including you!] *that he gave his one and only Son, that whoever believes in him shall not perish but have eternal life* (John 3:16). Jesus, God's one and only Son, died for sinners. What does this tell you about how much God loves you?

_____

_____

Allow God to lead you. Knowing God loves you requires a response from you. One key way you show your love for God is by doing what He wants you to do. Jesus tells us in the Bible how important doing His will is. He said:

If you love me, you will obey what I command (John 14:15). What does a heart that loves Jesus do?

_____

_____

As we've already discovered, a girl after God's own heart is a girl who will do what God wants her to do. Her thinking goes like this: "If God wants me to do this, I'm going to do it. And if God doesn't want me to do this, I'm not going to do it."

Are you wondering, "How? How can I know what God wants me to do? How can I be sure of what He wants?" Well, I have good news! God has already stated His will in His Word, the Bible. So be sure you set aside some time to read your Bible. If you're not sure about what you are reading, talk it over with your parents, pastors, or Sunday school teachers. God has given these people to you to guide you and help you understand what to do.

Your word is a lamp to my feet and a light for my path (Psalm 119:105). How will the Bible help you?

_____

_____

I have hidden your word in my heart that I might not sin against you (Psalm 119:11). How will learning and memorizing God's Word help you?

_____

_____

Remember, God wants you to love Him. Now think about some of the things you love. I hope your mom and dad pop into your mind. And maybe a best friend. Perhaps you thought of your new puppy, or a hobby like knitting, doing crafts, ice skating, swimming, ballet, music, or your doll collection. Or maybe playing sports like soccer or basketball or tennis. Or even things you love to eat like ice cream, chocolate, chips, and donuts—yum, yum!

Now it's time for you to make your list of "Things I Love":

_____

_____

_____

_____

_____

_____

Now—back to God! God wants you to love *Him*. In fact, He wants to be at the top of your "Things I Love" list. He wants you to love Him *more than* all other things. And He wants you to love Him with all your heart. Jesus says,

> *Love the Lord your God with all your heart and with all your soul and with all your mind* (Matthew 22:37). Circle every time the word "all" is used.

Love like this is a tall order, isn't it? But it is possible to love God more than anything else. All you have to do is choose to put Him first in your life and in your heart, one day at a time. Here are some ways to get started:

- When you go to bed at night, tell God that you love Him and that you are going to think about Him first thing as soon as you wake up. Then say, "Good night, Lord. I love You!"

- When you wake up, say, "Good morning!" to God.

It's just like King David said in Psalm 5:3: "My voice You shall hear in the morning, O LORD" (NKJV). Thank the Lord for His love, His blessings, all the good things in your life, and your brand-new day.

◉ I don't know about you, but when I was a girl, I dearly loved writing in my diary. It was a special, private place where I could share about my heart and my life. A lot of things happen in one day, things you don't want to forget. So write about them! But don't forget that the most important thing to write down is what you learned about God or Jesus, and how much you love Him. Try it! It will be just between you and God, a time to say, "Thank You for my special day, God."

Take the temperature of your heart. Throughout this book we'll talk a lot about your heart. But right now it's time to take the temperature of your heart. You already know how your mom takes your body temperature with a thermometer when you're not feeling well. That helps her know if you are sick or not. And, if you are sick, it helps her to know if you're a little sick or *really* sick!

Think about this scene from the book of Revelation. Jesus is speaking to the people in a certain church. Here's what He said to them:

I know your deeds, that you are neither cold nor hot. I wish you were either one or the other! So, because you are lukewarm—

neither hot nor cold—I am about to spit you out of my mouth (Revelation 3:15-16).

Jesus mentions three heart conditions or temperatures. List them here.

_____

_____

_____

To be *coldhearted* means to be unemotional, unaware of God. It's hard to imagine being a person who doesn't even think about God at all! To be *lukewarm* means to be indifferent and bored. Oh, dear! Imagine being numb toward God, bored about God! The third temperature—*hot!*—means that the heat of your heart and your emotions toward God is sky-high. That means your love for God is boiling over with emotion, excitement, and passion. It's fiery! It's the heart of someone—*you!*—who loves God and is committed to Him.

HEART 2 HEART

Just think about Jesus' love for a minute. He loved you so much that He died for you so that you could have eternal life and be with Him forever. And think about how He loved you before you ever loved Him. I hope your heart is as excited about Jesus right now as mine is. If it's not, I hope your heart will warm up, ignite, and begin to burn with a real love for Jesus.

All sorts of exciting and positive things can happen as you turn up the heat of your love for Jesus. So let's discover how you can understand a bit more about Jesus and His plan for you. But first, pray this prayer. Its words will tell Jesus of your desire to know and love Him more and more:

Dear Jesus, help me
to love You more,
to know You better,
and to follow You with all my heart.
Amen.

In this chapter we had some fun in God's Word learning about the importance of **H-E-A-R-T**. On this page, write out the point for each letter. (I'll get you started with "H.")

H ave a heart check-up.

E _____

A _____

R _____

T _____

Now, write out one thing you liked, learned, or want to do about your heart and your love for Jesus. Then enjoy the adventure!

_____

_____

_____

_____

_____

_____

2

My Space

Emma was beside herself with excitement. Her grandmother was coming for a visit! She could hardly wait to have her Mimi right in her house.

At last Mimi arrived. Even though Emma's mom had told her to give her grandmom a few minutes to get settled, Emma simply could not wait. As soon as she got a great big hug from her grandmom, she blurted out, "Mimi, Mimi, come see my room!"

Now it was Mimi's turn to get excited as Emma put a scarf over her eyes and carefully guided her into her bedroom. When Emma uncovered her eyes, Mimi squealed, "Emma, I can't believe my eyes! What a great room! I can only imagine all the fun you have here. It looks like the kind of place you would enjoy."

Emma was elated! It gave her such joy to show her Mimi her cozy bed and favorite cuddly blankets, her cool reading lamp clipped on the bed frame, and the special basket under the bed where she kept her library books, fun books, and diary. Emma even opened her beautiful "Keep

Out! Private!" box that she kept next to her pillow so Mimi could see her most treasured things.

FUN IN GOD'S WORD!

I'm sure you've watched your mom working hard to take care of the place where you and your family live. You've seen how she cleans, decorates, and cares for her home. Well, you can do the same things for your own little home sweet home. When you take care of your area of the house—whether it's your bunk in the bedroom you share with a sister or a bedroom all your own—you'll feel really great about it. And here's a bonus—you'll get good experience for the future God has planned for you.

To find out what a few of those plans are, get your hands on your favorite pen again! It's time to mark what you learn in the verses below about your S-P-A-C-E—your little home sweet home.

Show good character by taking care of your space. Remember our theme verse? It's Acts 13:22. A girl who wants to follow God is one who wants what God wants. She wants to do God's will. And she wants to please God. Did you ever think that a part of God's plan for you is learning to take care of your space? That's right! The Bible says,

> *Whatever you do, work at it with all your heart, as working for the Lord, not for men* (Colossians 3:23). As a tween girl, you don't have a "job" like an adult does. But you do

have your room. And you show good character qualities when you take care of it. *How* does this verse say you are to do your work, including taking care of your clothes and belongings? *Who* does this verse say you are working for?

_____

_____

_____

Pray and thank Jesus for your space. Like Emma, your space is important to you. It's your little "place." So take some time to describe your room. When you're done, don't forget to thank Jesus for the things you have and for a place and space of your own. The Bible says, "Be thankful" (Colossians 3:15).

_____

_____

_____

_____

_____

_____

_____

_____

_____

Acknowledge your duty. You can do lots of things with your time—watch TV, play video games, enjoy your doll collection, or play outside. But there's something else that requires your time—your room! And God is asking you to take care of this special place. He says:

> *She watches carefully all that goes on throughout her household, and is never lazy* (Proverbs 31:27 TLB). This verse describes the actions of a wise woman—and a wise girl—as she takes care of her home or her space. What does it say is the secret to taking care of your room?

_____

_____

Taking care of your place takes time. According to this verse, where does this time come from?

_____

_____

Clean freaks apply here. Please don't freak out as we talk about being a clean freak! Just think about this for a minute. Your room is *you*. If it's tidy, that tells people something about you and your character—that you are a neat person. You also send a message about yourself if your space is a real pigpen. What you want to be is neat and organized.

Take a look at the chart on the next page. First, I want you to circle every time the word "your" occurs in the chart. Next, make a check mark in the column that represents the person who usually does each of the following basic chores. If it's another person ("other"), write in their name for each task they do. When you're done, add up the check marks to see who's really taking care of *your* room.

TASK	YOU	MOM	OTHER
Vacuum your floor			
Dust your furniture			
Hang up your clothes			
Put away your clothes			
Wash your clothes			
Fold your clothes			
Put your folded clothes away			
Totals of check marks	_____	_____	_____

Now, take a look at your totals. What do you see? Who's doing most of *your* work?

Here's a challenge. Try being a "tidy freak" for a few days. I know, you'll probably have to pick your mom up off the floor during those few days! But I guarantee, you'll love the results. You'll feel so good about your room—and yourself. Why? Because you'll realize that *you* made your room neat and inviting! Here's a thought from God about being tidy and neat:

Everything should be done in...[an] orderly way (1 Corinthians 14:40). This verse gives us a general principle for life, including the way you live and take care of your things. What does it say about order and about being a neat freak?

_____

_____

_____

Express yourself in your space. When it comes to your room, I realize your mom probably has a lot to say about the color of your furniture and sheets, whether you have that cute rug you like or not, and what you hang on the walls. God wants you to listen to her and respect that.

There are good reasons why your mom says yes or no to your ideas. For instance, stuff for your room costs money. A wall that has holes in it from posters and pictures has to be patched and painted later on. And paint and carpet color choices may be dictated by the person your parents rent from, or by a general color scheme for the entire house.

Please realize you need to work *with* your mom when it comes to your room. Share your ideas. Go through magazines and show her pictures of what you like. Ask her for decorating advice. And if it's okay with your mom, cut out some magazine pictures and start a notebook for creating your dream room. When it comes to your mom's help, instruction, and advice about your room, the Bible has something to say to you:

The younger women...[are to be taught] to be busy at home (Titus 2:4-5). Who is the best person to teach you about taking care of your room?

_____

_____

 HEART 2 HEART

Did you ever think that the God of the universe would be interested in you and the things you do and don't do? Well, amazingly, He is! God is definitely interested in how you take care of your little home, your room, your space.

As you follow God's desire in this area, get ready for a *b-i-g* reward! You won't believe how good you will feel when you're done taking care of your room. When you look at your shiny room, at all your neat things, at the order, you will be pleased and proud of your efforts. You'll be glad you followed after God's own heart and followed His instruction. And you will be rewarded in your heart for what you have done.

In this chapter we had some fun in God's Word learning about the importance of **S-P-A-C-E.** On this page, write out the point for each letter. (I'll get you started with "S.")

S how good character by taking care of your space.

P _____

A _____

C _____

E _____

Now, write out one thing you liked, learned, or want to do about your space. Then enjoy the adventure!

_____

_____

_____

_____

_____

_____

_____

3

My Parents

Emma? Emma! Emma Thomas!" Oh dear! Emma was staring out the window at school—again. But this time she wasn't lost in thought about the upcoming "cool girl birthday party." No, this was way more serious. She was thinking about how much she missed her mom.

Now, before you get the wrong idea, understand that Mrs. Thomas is alive and well! What Emma was missing was *time* with her mom. Recently, her mom had taken on a work project. It was temporary, but still, Emma missed her. Why? Because her mom was Emma's best friend. They had such good times together. There was no one else Emma wanted to be with or talk to more than Mom.

But things had changed. Her mom worked afternoons and got home just in time to fix dinner, clean up, and get Emma and her brother and sister ready for bed. Her mother just didn't seem to have much time for her. As a result, Emma felt sad—and mad! She felt like she had lost her best friend! She didn't like it, and her attitude was bad. She was even beginning to talk back to her mom! Emma had always been eager to please and obey her parents, but her bitterness and confusion were causing her to sulk and refuse to follow even the most simple instructions from her parents.

FUN IN GOD'S WORD!

You probably hear many kids put their parents down, criticize them, and make fun of them. You've probably even heard them say things like, "My parents are so stupid. What do they know anyway?" If you listen to too much of this kind of talk, you'll begin to think that's how you are supposed to talk about *your* parents. I heard a lot of this when I was growing up. And I still hear a lot of it now. But I remember the day I looked at James 1:17 with my parents in mind. It was then I realized, "Wait a minute! *God* gave me my parents exactly the way they are and who they are. That means they are one of His gifts to me!"

I can't begin to tell you how this changed my attitude toward my mom and dad. Instead of seeing them as goofy, old-fashioned, too strict, and picky, I started seeing them as special gifts from God, just for me. And God would want you to have this same attitude about your parents.

Let's have some fun as we spell out the word P-A-R-E-N-T-S. Get your special pen or pencil ready, and let your adventure into God's Word continue!

Pray for your parents. Prayer is a wonderful habit. No matter where you are or what's happening, you can talk to God. God cares about you, and He cares about your parents too. Praying for your mom or dad is a good thing. It helps you to love and care for them even more. You can even make a special page in your journal or diary just for things you want to pray for regarding Mom and Dad.

Always [give] thanks to God the Father for everything (Ephesians 5:20). What is God telling you to do here? When are you to do it? Have you given thanks to God for your parents?

_____

_____

_____

_____

Always remember that giving thanks is a part of prayer. So don't forget to thank God every day for your very own special parents.

And don't forget to say thank you to your parents every day, all day long, for everything. Your parents do a lot for you. If they buy you new clothes, tell them thank you. If you attend ballet or gymnastics classes or are on a sports team, say thank you. When you eat a meal, say thank you. When clean clothes magically show up in your drawers, say thank you. And when you go to bed, say, "Thank you, Mom and Dad, for another great day!"

Ask their advice. God gave you your parents. And guess what? They can help you make good decisions, give you great advice, and guide you in the right direction. They have wisdom to share. (Yes, they too had to grow up!) And most of all, they love you and want the best for you. No one loves you more than your parents do—except for God, of course!

Once your parents give you advice or make a rule or a decision, it's important to do what they say. One time my parents said *no* when I asked them if I could go to a slumber party. I was so mad because I so wanted to be a part of the excitement—and the group! I cried, I whined, I begged, and I thought horrible things about my parents. But would you believe a bunch of boys showed up at the house where the sleepover was? Then the kids got so loud that the neighbors called the police, who came over too. Wow, was I ever glad my parents said no!

Usually, if your attitude is right, you can talk things over with your parents. You can ask them why they made a certain decision. You can ask them what you need to do to earn a privilege. In the end, though, you want to do what they say—with a happy heart.

Listen, my [child], to your father's instruction and do not forsake your mother's teaching (Proverbs 1:8). What is God's advice regarding your father and your mother?

_____

_____

Respect your parents. Think for a minute about your teachers at school. You answer when they call on you.

You do whatever they ask. And you wouldn't argue with them. Well, why would you show such respect for a teacher you see for a few hours each week, and choose *not* to treat your parents the same way? Why would you submit to authority at school, but not at home? Once again, Jesus has something to say about this:

> *Honor your father and mother* (Matthew 15:4). What is Jesus' clear and simple command to you?

_____

_____

Did you know that, when Jesus said these words, He was talking about one of the Ten Commandments? That makes this a very important thing to remember, doesn't it? What does it mean to respect your parents? It means to treat them politely and with honor. It means to admire them. It means to listen when they talk. It means to accept their decisions, follow their rules, and seek to please them. And it means you don't talk back or argue!

Experience God's blessing through obedience. Each one of us is an individual with a mind of our own. We have ideas about the way we want to do things. How do we know if what we want to do is the right thing to do? God gave you your parents to help you make the right decisions at each stage of your life. Just as you want your parent's approval, you should also want God's approval. How do you receive God's approval or blessing? These verses tell you how. (And don't miss the promise that goes with the blessing!)

Children, obey your parents in the Lord, for this is right (Ephesians 6:1). What is God's command to you? Why should you obey your parents?

_____

_____

_____

Honor your father and mother...that it may go well with you (Ephesians 6:2-3). What is God's command to you, and what is one result of doing this?

_____

_____

_____

Never criticize your parents to others. This is a part of God's command that you honor your father and mother. So be careful not to criticize someone you love, respect, and honor. You should be very careful not to put down your parents when you talk to other people. Instead, you are to speak well of your parents. Once again, no matter how popular it is for kids to talk badly about their parents, you shouldn't. Why?

A foolish [person] *despises his mother* (Proverbs 15:20). To "despise" means to mock and to have no respect.

How does God describe a son or daughter who despises their mother?

_____

_____

Trust God. It takes trust in God to listen to your parents and do what they say. You have to trust God that He is leading and growing you through your parents. No matter what happens, you can always trust God.

Trust in the LORD with all your heart and lean not on your own understanding; in all your ways acknowledge him, and he will make your paths straight (Proverbs 3:5-6). What is God's promise to you if you will trust and follow Him with all your heart?

_____

_____

_____

_____

_____

Say, "I love you." Isn't it great when your parents say, "I love you" or show their love to you? And you love them as much as they love you, right? So why not tell them you love them—often? And love isn't just words you say. It's also action and behavior. Read on!

Dear children, let us not love with words or tongue but with actions and in truth (1 John 3:18). In addition to saying, "I love you," how do you prove you love your parents?

_____

_____

HEART 2 HEART

Let's go back to Emma once again. Remember how confused and upset she was with the change in her relationship with her mom? So what did Emma do? She began to do things like not obeying and not showing respect.

Now, think—who was Emma hurting? For sure, she was probably hurting her mom. But according to what we just learned from the Bible, who else would be disappointed? *God* is the right answer.

A girl after God's own heart follows God's instruction to honor her parents. Do you remember our theme verse—Acts 13:22? It tells us that a girl after God's own heart is a girl who will do everything God wants her to do. If you've been mean to your parents, it's time for a change of heart. Tell God what's been going on and ask for His forgiveness. Tell God you're sorry and ask for His help. And tell Him you want to follow His Word and love, honor, and obey your parents.

And then take the final step—do it! Make the changes you need to make! Pray and work on having a happy, obedient heart in all things, and see what a wonderful difference that makes at home with your parents.

In this chapter we had some fun in God's Word learning about the importance of **P-A-R-E-N-T-S.** On this page, write out the point for each letter. (I'll get you started with "P.")

P ray for your parents.

A _____

R _____

E _____

N _____

T _____

S _____

Now, write out one thing you liked, learned, or want to do about being a better daughter. Then enjoy the adventure!

_____

_____

_____

4

My Family

Get out of my room, you little brat!" yelled Brittany, Emma's sister. Brittany was five years older than Emma, and it seemed like she lived on a different planet. Emma loved her dolls and stuffed animals, but Brittany was into clothes, music, friends, and especially boys. Ugh!

Brittany *was* pretty. And it's true she did wear really neat clothes. And yes, she had cool friends. Emma adored Brittany and looked up to her. She wanted more than anything to spend lots and lots of time with her big sis. But it seemed like Brittany had determined to take every opportunity to be mean to Emma and their little brother, Pete. Whenever Brittany was around, Emma and Pete couldn't seem to do anything right. Brittany considered herself to be the princess of the family, and Emma and Pete were there to serve her—or else get out of her way!

Yes, Emma felt like she was living a modern-day version of Cinderella, except Brittany wasn't a stepsister. And she definitely wasn't ugly! Why did Brittany have to be so mean? Why couldn't they just be friends?

FUN IN GOD'S WORD!

It's pen or pencil time again! This time we're going on an adventure to discover what God tells us about our family members. As you have fun with the acrostic below that spells out F-A-M-I-L-Y, keep your pen handy. As you read, ask God for some good ideas about being a better family member.

Family is first. There is nothing as special as a family. Over the years your friends will come and go, but you will always have your family. And believe it or not, the day *will* come when you and your brothers and sisters will actually get along with each other and *want* to spend lots of time together.

Since family is your top priority (after God, that is), you need to make a decision to be loyal to your siblings. You can support your little brother in his soccer or T-ball efforts. The same is true for a big sister's swim meets or piano recitals. And after the game or activity, don't forget to tell them what a great job they did. Or, if they didn't get to play or it didn't go so well, give them a pat on the back and say, "I'm still proud of you. Your day will come." Be supportive in as many ways as you can.

A friend loves at all times, and a brother is born for adversity (Proverbs 17:17). Now read this verse again and say or think the word "sister" instead of "friend" or "brother." That's you! This verse is explaining how important family is when someone is suffering. How often does a friend or sister love her family? Even when things get tough, what is God asking of you as a friend or family member?

_____

_____

_____

_____

Ask God for help. It's hard to understand, but praying for others, including a stuck-up older sister, changes your heart. It's easy to fight with or yell at your brother or sister. It's easy to say mean things to them. And it's easy to call them names. Praying for them can be hard—especially if your feelings have been hurt, or you've been ignored or treated badly. But go ahead and ask God to help you love them, no matter what. Ask Him to help you be kind, even when they're mean. It's hard to pray for someone and hate them at the same time. Soon you'll discover you have a bit more patience with them and your feelings will turn to love.

Jesus has advice that will help you and your heart:

I tell you: Love your enemies and pray for those who persecute you (Matthew 5:44). What are the two steps Jesus asks of you?

◎

◎

Mean attitudes must go. I'm sure you've been on the receiving end of jokes, teasing, and name-calling. Well, you can't control what others say and do, but you are totally in control of what *you* say and do! You can choose to be mean and make fun of others—or not. You can decide to laugh at others and put them down—or not. And guess what? The best place to start being nice is at home.

You can't make others be nice to you or to each other, but you can be sure *you* don't act in the wrong ways to others. You can make sure you don't hurt your brothers and sisters through your words or actions. You can help your brothers and sisters feel better. God says:

> *Do not let any unwholesome talk come out of your mouths, but only what is helpful for building others up* (Ephesians 4:29). What are God's rules for your mouth and what you say to others?

◎ Do not speak what is...

◎ Do speak what is...

◎ Why?

Initiate a change in your attitude. There is a scary story in the Old Testament about two brothers, Cain and Abel. Cain was angry with his brother because God liked Abel's offering better than Cain's offering. Listen in now on God's talk with Cain about his attitude:

The LORD said to Cain, "Why are you angry?...sin is crouching at your door; it desires to have you, but you must master it" (Genesis 4:6-7). How did God describe Cain's anger? What did God tell him to do about his angry attitude?

_____

_____

_____

Now here's the scary part. Cain didn't do what God said to do. Cain did not change his attitude. Instead, "Cain attacked his brother Abel and killed him" (verse 8). God's message to your heart is this: The next time you get mad at a brother or sister, remember Cain. And do what God told Cain to do—control your bad attitude before it controls you!

Love your brothers and sisters, no matter what. When it comes to love, Emma had the right idea. Even though Brittany was mean to her and Pete, Emma still loved her older sister and wanted to be with her. Emma's love was not based on any nice things Brittany did for her. In fact, it was just the opposite. In spite of Brittany's actions, Emma still loved her.

How about you? Do you have this kind of love for your family members, especially your brothers and sisters? It's the kind of love God wants you to have, a love that is not based on the actions of others, but a love that comes from God's love for you. Take a look at these verses:

A new command I give you: Love one another. As I have loved you, so you must love one another (John 13:35). Love is so important to God that He commands us to love each other, especially our brothers and sisters. How—and how much—does Jesus say you are to love your family members?

_____

_____

_____

Your response to your family is important to God. Are you beginning to see a theme in this acrostic of F-A-M-I-L-Y? *You* are in control of your attitudes. You can be nice and sweet—or you can be hateful and hurtful. The choice is all yours.

Do you remember how we talked about speaking well of your parents in a previous chapter? We learned how important it is that you not talk about them in a negative way, that you not put them down or make fun of them to others. Well, the same is true about your brothers and sisters. You can respond to them with kindness and love. And you can speak well of them to others.

Be kind and compassionate to one another, forgiving each other, just as in Christ God forgave you (Ephesians 4:32). List three actions and attitudes you are to have toward others, including your brothers and sisters.

◎

◎

◎

HEART 2 HEART

Family members should adopt the motto of the Three Musketeers—"All for one and one for all." How can you help to make your home a better place for your family? It starts with you being a sister who is there for her parents and brothers and sisters. It starts with you thinking of others, encouraging others, and loving your family members. So make your move!

Got a big brother? Write him a note of thanks for being a super big brother and slip it under his door. Got a big sister? See if there's anything you can help her with in her busy schedule. Got a little brother? Help him, play with him, laugh with him, hug him, and encourage him. Got a little sister? Get involved in her life. Say, "Want to play?" or "Here, let me help you."

Now, here's a thought: Maybe you are the older sister. Are you being a "Brittany," or are you being God's helpful, kind big sis? Unfortunately Emma's big sister was so involved in herself that she failed to notice how much Emma wanted to spend time with her. I hope and pray you aren't living in your own world so much that you ignore your younger siblings. A girl after God's own heart is also a sister after God's own heart. What can you do today to love your brothers and sisters?

In this chapter we had some fun in God's Word learning about the importance of **F-A-M-I-L-Y**. On this page, write out the point for each letter. (I'll get you started with "F.")

F amily is first.

A _____

M _____

I _____

L _____

Y _____

Now, write out one thing you liked, learned, or want to do about being a better sister. Then enjoy the adventure!

_____
_____
_____
_____
_____

5

My School

When it came to school, Emma felt like two different people. Anything having to do with Mrs. Abrams was *the* most exciting thing in the world to her. Whatever Mrs. Abrams said or even hinted at, Emma rushed with great delight to do her best. But beyond her favorite teacher and her favorite subject—English—Emma wasn't that excited about school. Math was too hard. History was too boring. Science was too confusing. The one other bright spot in Emma's day was gym class, where she loved to play basketball, volleyball, and even softball when the weather was nice.

And after school? All that homework—ugh! All Emma wanted to do after school was kick back and relax with a snack and some down time in front of the TV with her little brother Pete. Or romp around the neighborhood with some of her best friends, who were homeschooled. But her most favorite thing to do was get together with several other neighborhood girls who were in a secret writing club that met after school in her friend Stephanie's tree house.

"Emma? Emma Elaine! Are you doing your homework yet?" Uh-oh! It was Mom calling Emma back to reality!

FUN IN GOD'S WORD!

I think all girls look forward to being older. Maybe that's why we love birthdays! All those presents, and the bonus of being a little older and more grown-up. But with each new year comes more responsibility, like taking school more seriously. School is an important part of growing up. It requires dedication, commitment, and time, but it can also be really exciting and fun!

I want you to have some fun now with the acrostic below that spells out S-C-H-O-O-L. Before we begin, here's something to remember if you're struggling with school and schoolwork—you can ask God for an attitude change.

See school as a training ground for life. Whether you attend a public school, a private school, or you are home-schooled, school is made up of lots of different things. The physical location and the time you spend there provide many opportunities for your growth. Just think about the many wonderful skills you develop at school.

- At school you have many opportunities to talk to and work with teachers, classmates, and friends.

- At school you learn how to ask and answer questions, give reports and presentations, and talk to a group.

⊚ At school you also learn to think and find solutions to problems and challenges.

⊚ At school you learn to act in a proper way toward those in authority and toward your fellow students. Also, being in school teaches you to restrain your emotions—and your mouth!—and to focus your active mind and energy.

Are you amazed? Are you getting a little bit better understanding about why school is so important? I hope so! Here's something from the Bible to help you with your attitude toward school.

If you look for [wisdom] as for silver and search for it as for hidden treasure, then you will understand the fear of the LORD *and find the knowledge of God* (Proverbs 2:4-5). Circle the words that describe the wealth and value of wisdom. Then underline the words that describe what you must do to get wisdom and knowledge. What is the result of gaining wisdom?

_____

_____

_____

_____

Check your attitude. Have you ever heard the saying, "Attitude is everything"? Well, I think that definitely applies to school. No matter where you go to school, you can make your time there whatever you want it to be. It can be fun and exciting, something you will look back on with wonderful memories—or it can be a living nightmare! And the amazing thing is that *you* get to choose which it will be!

Your happiness and success in school begin with your attitude. Can you say, "I'm going to make my school years fun, exciting, and meaningful"? I have a favorite quote I want to pass on to you. It says, "Wherever you are, be all there."[1] Since you have to "be" at school, why not decide to "be all there"? Maybe this verse will help!

> *Whatever you do, work at it with all your heart, as working for the Lord, not for men* (Colossians 3:23). How are you to do all your work, including going to school?

_____

_____

_____

_____

Homework is a priority. Of course, God is your Number One priority. Your whole life involves Him and revolves around Him. He is to be the most important person or thing in your life. But one of His major priorities for you is that you learn and grow by going to school and doing your homework. God's will for you at this time in your life is to be a student—to go to school, to learn as much as you can.

If you're like most of the girls I know, getting started on anything—including doing your homework—is the hardest part of any task. There just seem to be so many more exciting things to do! But to get your homework done, you have to get started. God has a few hints on how to do this—and with the right attitude!

Make every effort to add to your faith goodness; and to goodness, knowledge; and to knowledge, self-control, and to self-control, perseverance... (2 Peter 1:5-6). What do the first three words in these verses say is the very first thing you must do to get your homework done?

_____

_____

As you can see, growth requires something from you—effort and hard work! And the effort you make will pay off big-time as one good quality after another becomes a part of your life.

Organize for success. School is a place for learning. But to learn well, you need to be organized. One thing you'll need to do for school success is to set up a special place for doing your homework. Of course, you'll want Mom's approval of the place you pick. But wherever it is, try to make it a place you want to be. Think about special pencils and pens—and cool erasers! Ask Mom for a cute timer or clock so you can try to finish your homework by a certain time.

Next, pick a consistent time for doing your homework. I know girls who do some of their homework while they're at the bus stop. Or while they're waiting on the steps at school for their ride home. Or while they're at their grandmother's house while Mom is on her way home from work. Or even while sitting around the kitchen table all morning long with brothers and sisters while they're being home-schooled. Whatever works for you and your family, that will be your time. And here's a hint—sooner is better! Do your "work" (as in homework) first. *Then* do crafts, watch TV, or go to that secret girls' get-together.

I'm a writer. So far I've written almost 60 books. How did this happen? It happened because every day I go to my desk (my place where all my favorite things are) at a certain time (my time). Then I stay there until I write five pages.

My best friend is an artist. So far she has painted about 100 pictures. How did this happen? It happened because every day she goes to her work space (her place where all her neat art supplies are) at a certain time (her time). Then she stays there until she has done her work for the day.

My young friend, I will tell you that the years and years—and years!—of doing homework in a certain place, at a certain time, prepared both Judy and me for what we do now.

Other pursuits are a part of school. School offers many opportunities to get involved in different activities like sports or music. Maybe you're not so good at running races, but the swim team is where you fit. Or, if you're not interested in physical activities, how about the math club or the theater group? God has given you some super creative skills and natural talents. With your parents' permission, try anything and everything until you find your special "thing."

Jesus grew in wisdom and stature, and in favor with God and men (Luke 2:52). List the four areas of Jesus' development from a child to an adult. (And guess what? You need to grow in these same areas too!)

◎

◎

◎

◎

Listen to your parents. By all means, listen to your parents! They know all about doing homework. They also know all about what it takes to be a student—the discipline, the effort, the hard work, the time, the faithfulness and commitment. So ask them what school was like for them. Ask them about their favorite subjects—and why. Ask them to tell you about their favorite teachers—and why. This will be one fun conversation! You can even write down their answers right here!

My mom's/dad's favorite class in school, and why—

_____

_____

_____

_____

My mom's/dad's favorite teacher in school, and why—

_____

_____

_____

_____

I've said all along the way that you should do what your parents say. So, do your homework *when* they want you to do it. And be faithful to do it. That's one way to earn the privilege of being on a team or taking part in some after-school activities. And remember—sooner is better when it comes to getting your homework out of the way. As you read the verse below, think about how important learning and your daily schoolwork are.

Let the wise listen and add to their learning (Proverbs 1:5). What does the wise girl do?

_____

_____

_____

HEART 2 HEART

Are you catching a glimpse of God's plan for you to learn and grow? Are you catching on that your school-work is an important part of your grand adventure through life? I hope you are!

But it's also important to realize that as a girl after God's own heart, your relationship with Jesus is *the* most important thing. It's a good thing to go to school, work hard, do your homework, and get good grades. Just be sure you are also taking care of your walk with Jesus. That's because *the* L*ORD* *gives wisdom, and from his mouth comes knowledge and understanding* (Proverbs 2:6).

In this chapter we had some fun in God's Word learning about the importance of S-C-H-O-O-L. On this page, write out the point for each letter. (I'll get you started with "S.")

S chool is made up of lots of different things.

C _____

H _____

O _____

O _____

L _____

Now, write out one thing you liked, learned, or want to do about your time at school and doing your homework. Then enjoy the adventure!

_____

_____

_____

_____

6

My Friends

Jenny had been Emma's best friend from the day Emma's family moved in next door to Jenny's family. Both Emma and Jenny were five years old then. They started first grade together. They learned to read and write together. They shared books and read each other's personal dreams in their diaries. They had always been together and best buddies—until the day Tiffany started being nice to Emma.

Emma couldn't believe that Tiffany and her cool-girl friends would want to be friends with her. But they did! There were only two problems with Emma's friendship with the cool-girl crowd. The first was that Jenny was not included, which meant Emma had to make a choice between spending time with Jenny or with her new group of friends. The second was the way the cool girls treated the not-so-cool girls, including Jenny. They were mean and thought they were way better than the other girls in their grade. Emma felt uncomfortable with their awful attitudes and actions. She was beginning to realize that if she didn't act like them, they would exclude her. Hmmm. That would make Emma a nobody again.

FUN IN GOD'S WORD!

Friends. Sometimes it seems like you can't live *with* them, and sometimes it seems like you can't live *without* them! Friends are definitely an important part of your life, aren't they? Friends make life more fun and interesting. Friends help you grow in your communication skills as you talk—and talk—and talk some more! Friends also help you develop many strong character qualities. For example, you learn the importance of telling the truth and not spreading gossip, and you learn what it means to be loyal.

I'm sure you're seeing how important it is that you choose your friends carefully. You must try to choose friends who help you to grow into a girl after God's own heart. And at the same time, you have to be a true and real friend to others. Are you ready to work your magic with your pen as we see what God says about this important area of your life—F-R-I-E-N-D-S?

Friends love at all times. Can you relate in any way to the story of Emma and Jenny? Are you having to choose between a tried-and-true friend like Jenny and a new friend? Maybe you and your longtime friend are now at different schools, and it's hard to stay close and connected. I read a story about two girls who were best friends. They enjoyed the same things, laughed at the same jokes, and shared the same love for the color purple—and for French fries! They were like twin sisters—always together. When they were no longer placed in the same class, they had to work hard to remain friends.

What did they do? They made sure they talked on the phone—a lot! They got together at one or the other's house often. They signed up for the church youth program and memorized their Bible verses together. And they wrote notes to each other every day. They lived out this verse from the Bible:

> *A friend loves at all times, and a brother [or sister] is born for adversity* (Proverbs 17:17). Describe what a true friend does. When is a friend most needed?

_____

_____

_____

_____

Refuse to be a part of a clique. A clique is an exclusive group of people who spend all their time together and don't allow others to join them. At school or church, these are the girls who sit together, walk together, talk to each other, and generally have nothing to do with anyone else. They may even dress alike or have the same style of hair.

Now, there's nothing wrong with having a group of friends that have similar things in common. The problem comes when the group becomes mean and exclusive and believes they are better, prettier, and more "with it" than outsiders.

Is this the kind of group you want to be a part of? I don't think so, even if (like Emma) you consider yourself a "nobody." Remember, you are a "somebody" to Jesus! We can learn a lesson from Jesus. He was a friend to all, yet He was criticized because He ate and drank and talked with the wrong people people who were considered to be "sinners" or were rejected by others.

Like Jesus, you probably know how it feels to be avoided, ignored, excluded, and overlooked by others. So what can you do?

- Grow in God, and you won't mind the cliques so much. Also, as you are growing in Christ, you will attract other friends who want to be more like Jesus.

- Pray for God to bring a godly friend into your life, and pray for the people in the mean group.

- Be friendly to everyone, and be thankful for the friends you have. Also, be a true friend to your true friends!

Initiate friendships carefully. Choose your friends wisely. Why? Because you become what they are. That's why the Bible is very clear when it tells you what to look for in a friend—and also what to avoid at all costs. Seek out friends who are going in the right direction spiritually—toward Jesus. What do these friends look like? You will know them because they will pull you along in your journey with Jesus and pull you up in your love for Jesus. Where will you find friends like this? You will usually find them at church or in Christian groups or activities.

He who walks with the wise grows wise, but a companion of fools suffers harm (Proverbs 13:20). If your friends are wise, what happens to you? If your friends are fools, what happens to you?

_____

_____

_____

Everyone deserves your friendliness. I hope you are getting God's message about how important it is to choose friends and friendships carefully. But this caution should not scare you away from being friendly to all. What does it mean to be friendly? Try living by the "Ten Commandments of Friendship."[2]

1. Speak to people—there is nothing as nice as a cheerful word of greeting.

2. Smile at people—it takes seventy-two muscles to frown and only fourteen to smile!

3. Call people by name—the sweetest music to anyone's ear is the sound of their own name.

4. Be friendly and helpful—if you would have friends, be friendly.

5. Be cordial—speak and act as if everything you do were a real pleasure.

6. Be genuinely interested in people—you can like *everyone* if you try.

7. Be generous with praise—cautious with criticism.

8. Be considerate of the feelings of others—it will be appreciated.

9. Be thoughtful of the opinions of others.

10. Be alert to give service—what counts most in life is what we do for others!

Nice is always in. So be nice! Have you ever heard of the Golden Rule? It says, "Do to others as you would have them do to you." Did you know that Jesus was the person who taught that? (see Luke 6:31). The Golden Rule is an important reason for being nice to others because we want them to be nice to us! But did you know that the Bible never tells us to just be nice? Here's what it says instead:

Be kind and compassionate to one another (Ephesians 4:32). How are you to treat anybody and everybody?

_____

_____

_____

Are you wondering, "So what's the difference?" Well, here it is. Being nice is just being polite. But being kind is being caring and thoughtful. As you probably know, you can "act" nice toward someone even when you really can't stand them! But being kind is a deep, sincere, heartfelt action. Here is another verse about being kind:

Love is patient, love is kind (1 Corinthians 13:4). How do you show love to others?

_____

_____

Don't gossip! Real friends don't tell secrets or spread rumors about their friends. A true friend is loyal and knows how to keep a secret. The Bible has a *lot* to say about gossip and how it harms friendships.

Whoever spreads slander is a fool (Proverbs 10:18). It's easy to get the meaning of this verse! Don't gossip and spread rumors about others. If you do, what does this verse say about you?

_____

_____

A talebearer reveals secrets, but he who is of a faithful spirit conceals a matter (Proverbs 11:13 NKJV). What does a talebearer or a gossip do? What does a faithful friend do instead?

_____

_____

_____

_____

If you've ever been hurt by gossip, you know the meaning of this proverb all too well! So don't gossip. You're supposed to be a *friend* to others, not someone who hurts others by sharing secrets or lies about them. To share someone's secrets is to betray a friend. It hurts your friendships. And guess what else? It hurts you! Instead, you are to be loyal, trustworthy, and true-hearted—a *real* friend.

Share Jesus with your friends. If you have a personal relationship with Jesus, then you have a friend in Jesus. He is the truest friend you could ever have and will ever have (John 15:15). Because Jesus is the best friend any girl could have, you want to tell others about Him, right? Briefly write out what Jesus means to you. Then pray for a chance to share with your friends what you have written.

_____

_____

_____

_____

_____

_____

_____

_____

_____

HEART 2 HEART

I'm sure you realize the importance of friends and especially the right kind of friends. The right kind of friend will encourage you in the Lord. She will challenge you in your spiritual growth and your adventure with Jesus. In fact, she'll be right there by your side enjoying the adventure with Jesus! And she will stay with you even during the tough times. So as you go about the business of looking for a friend, start with prayer. Here's a prayer you can say. Or feel free to make up your own. Whatever you pray, pray it from your heart.

A PRAYER FOR FRIENDS

Dear Lord and Father,

I pray for my social life and my friends. Bring friends into my life who will love and encourage me, who will bring joy and laughter in the good times and comfort and support through difficulties and disappointments. Grant me wisdom as I seek true friends. I ask that You fill my life with close and caring relationships. Amen.[3]

In this chapter we had some fun in God's Word learning about the importance of **F-R-I-E-N-D-S**. On this page, write out the point for each letter. (I'll get you started with "F.")

F riends love at all times.

R _____

I _____

E _____

N _____

D _____

S _____

Now, write out one thing you liked, learned, or want to do about your friendships and being a better friend. Then enjoy the adventure!

_____

_____

7

My Church

"Wouldn't it be nice to sleep in just *one* day of the week?" Emma said to herself as she turned over in bed to catch another snooze. But Emma's mom made sure that Sunday was not going to be a sleep-in day. She was making the rounds, waking up Emma and her brother and sister. Emma sighed as she heard her mom's voice: "Emma? Emma Elaine! Get up N-O-W!"

Emma rolled out of bed and staggered to the window. All was quiet. Then she smiled as it hit her—*Sunday at last!* She had packed her Bible and Sunday school lesson the night before. Plus she had set out her church outfit and her cool new shoes.

Emma was getting more and more excited each minute about going to church. This hadn't always been true. But recently, Sundays had become the highlight of Emma's week because of Jill, her new Sunday school teacher. Jill was a student at the local college who loved Jesus and enjoyed teaching the Bible to fifth- and sixth-grade girls. Jill's obvious love for the Lord had lit a spiritual fire in Emma's heart.

"Thank You, Jesus, for Jill!" Emma prayed as she rushed down the stairs to breakfast. Sunday at last!

FUN IN GOD'S WORD!

At church, you can have fun with your friends and the other kids in your Sunday school class. And if you have a teacher like Jill, you can learn a lot about Jesus and being a girl after God's own heart. Also, church is where you and your family can worship God together. Church is just a good place to be!

If you're like most of the girls I know, though, some Sundays roll around and you just don't feel like getting up and getting dressed to go anywhere. Who doesn't like lounging around in their pj's and eating pancakes? But going to church is something God wants you and me to do. It's a great place to hear His Word, to learn about Him, and to learn how He wants us to live.

Now it's time for some more fun in God's Word. And you know what to do, right? Let's see what God has to say about your involvement at C-H-U-R-C-H.

Church is God's plan. In the Old Testament, God asked His people to worship Him in a specific *place* like a tabernacle (a tent) or a temple. But in the New Testament, God built His church out of *people*. So the church is not a building. It's a group of people who believe in Christ as their Lord.

Christ loved the church and gave himself up for her (Ephesians 5:25). How important is the church to Jesus?

_____

_____

Have a positive attitude. When it comes to going to church, pray that you will pay attention. Try to get everything you can from your teacher's lesson. Participate in the discussion. If a lesson was assigned in advance, be sure to do it.

> Worship the LORD with gladness; come before him with joyful songs...Enter his gates with thanksgiving and his courts with praise; give thanks to him and praise his name (Psalm 100:2 and 4). In these verses, circle at least four attitudes for worshiping God.

When you attend church and your youth group with an eager and open heart, you bring glory to God. That's awesome!

Understand the importance of youth activities. Church is not school, and it's not home. It's a special place provided by God for His special people—those who love Him—to get together.

Most churches have Bible clubs where you can play games, memorize Scripture, talk about Jesus, and have fun with other kids your age. Your church might also offer special day camps or weekend camps where you can get away and be with other kids and leaders who love Jesus. My personal favorite was the annual winter camp. I loved going up to the mountains and rolling around in the snow. And I loved gathering around a fireplace later to warm up and hear my youth leader talk about the most important person in the world—Jesus! And how about summer camp—staying in a cabin, swimming every day, and going on nature hikes?

So, if it's at all possible, don't miss out on these church activities. The things you do and learn and the commitments you make during these times can be some of the most important and memorable ones you make in your entire life. Plus, you can make some great, genuine friendships with other girls who love Jesus, too.

There's a story in the Bible that tells about the special time Jesus spent with His disciples. He told them,

> *Come with me by yourselves to a quiet place* (Mark 6:31). How does that verse encourage you to attend the next church youth activity (with your parents' approval, of course)?

_____

_____

_____

Reach out to other girls. Church is full of kids who love Jesus and want to know more about Him and His Word. As I've heard all my life, "The ground is level at the foot of the cross." In Christ, we are all one. Underline what these verses say about how Christ makes us equal.

> *There is neither Jew nor Greek, slave nor free, male nor female, for you are all one in Christ Jesus* (Galatians 3:28).

Here are some things you can do to reach out to others in your class at church. You can easily do every one of these acts of friendliness. All it takes to make them happen is your decision to do them!

- ◎ Say hi to everyone—and smile.

- ◎ Sit by any girl who is alone. If you're with a friend, both of you can go sit with her.

- ◎ If someone is new or a visitor, be sure to say hello. Ask her where she lives or who she's visiting and how long she'll be there. Be friendly!

Christ is what church is all about. Jesus is what makes going to church different from going to school or gymnastics class. It is His church. And you go there to learn about Him.

Your parents may talk about Jesus at home and have devotions together as a family. But church is another place where you can learn more about Jesus and His amazing life and miracles. You'll read about His love and character qualities. You'll find out how He expects you to act and behave. You'll love learning about what Jesus has done for you, that He died for you and for sin. And you'll hear about the way to enjoy eternal life in heaven forever.

Many Christians I know gave their hearts and lives to Jesus at church as they discovered more about the Lord. The most important decision you will ever make is whether you will follow Jesus and whether you will give Him your heart and life. I'm praying that God will use His Word to open your heart to the truth of His love for you, that you will respond to His invitation to "come unto Me."

You'll read more about becoming a Christian and what's at the heart of an adventure with Jesus in chapter 10. But for now, what does this verse tell you about Jesus?

Jesus answered, "I am the way and the truth and the life. No one comes to the Father except through me" (John 14:6).

_____

_____

_____

Help in any and every way. Church is sometimes called "the body of Christ." People in the body of Christ help one another—and *you* can, too! If cupcakes are needed for your class at church, ask your mom if she can help you bake some. If help is needed to set up the classroom or clean up afterward, ask Mom and Dad if it's okay to go a little early or stay a few minutes late so you can help out.

You can also help your parents with their ministries. I know a mom and dad who volunteer to take care of the babies in the church nursery—and their kids gladly help them after church is over. Their Katie (age 9) helps clean and put away the toys and equipment, rolls up rugs, and vacuums the floor.

Or here's another way you can help. When there's a church workday, ask your dad if you can go along with him.

It's really fun to plant and water flowers, sweep up leaves, and help make the church look nice.

What you want to develop is a heart that serves. That's one way you can be more like Jesus.

Even the Son of Man did not come to be served, but to serve, and to give his life as a ransom for many (Mark 10:45). What does this verse tell you about Jesus?

_____

_____

_____

 HEART 2 HEART

Emma was glad. She had Jill! And Jill made being at church fun and exciting. But maybe you don't have a Jill. This might mean you will need to make more of an effort to grow spiritually and learn more about Jesus while you're at church. And, as we've discovered, part of that learning comes with going to church and being a part of youth activities.

And just think of the neat things that happen to you while you're at church. For one, you are set apart from the world and its negative influences for a few hours. And you get to be in a place where the kids are thinking and talking about Jesus. You can build friendships with girls who have the same priorities you have. And who knows? Someday in the way distant future, in God's timing, you might even meet a cool boy who thinks about Jesus like you do!

I hope and pray you love going to church. And if you're not exactly "loving" the idea of going to church, I hope and pray you'll have a change of heart. Ask God to help you understand how important it is to meet with Christians and grow in the Lord. You can always pray to meet a new friend there, too—a sister-in-Christ after God's own heart whom you can look forward to seeing each week.

So, to sum things up, here are four good reasons to enjoy and appreciate your time at church. Each one is important, and each one is an exciting reason to want to go to church. You go to church...

- to worship Jesus.
- to be taught more about Jesus.
- to bring kids who need to know Jesus.
- to serve others like Jesus.

In this chapter we had some fun in God's Word learning about the importance of C-H-U-R-C-H. On this page, write out the point for each letter. (I'll get you started with "C.")

C hurch is God's plan.

H _____

U _____

R _____

C _____

H _____

Now, write out one thing you liked, learned, or want to do about your involvement at your church. Then enjoy the adventure!

_____

_____

_____

_____

8

My Self

"Wow! Oh, wow!" That was all Emma could say. She was absolutely overwhelmed! She and her mom had just stepped into the civic auditorium, where the annual county craft fair was being held. This was the first time Emma's mom had invited her to the fair. (Well, her mom had invited her last year, but at the time she was more interested in playing with the neighborhood kids.)

But this year was different. Over the years, Emma had watched her mom create gifts for others. Now she was excited to start learning how to make such cool crafts. And she was excited about this special time together with her mom!

As Emma stood there, she couldn't help but reflect on how things were changing in her life, in her interests, her body, and her dreams. With each passing year, her schoolwork was getting more demanding. As her friends grew older and changed too, it was becoming more difficult to have real friendships. And she couldn't quite figure out what was going on, but she had noticed she was getting more moody. At times she felt as if she were on a roller coaster of emotions. Things that once were fun weren't quite so fun anymore. It seemed like life had become more complicated.

Well, thank goodness for the craft fair! The thrilling sight of the many craft booths quickly erased all of Emma's worries and concerns as she wondered, "Now, which booth should I visit first? Wow! Oh, wow!"

FUN IN GOD'S WORD!

Some parts of growing up are tons of fun. To begin with, there are lots of great new things to do almost every day. And as you grow physically, guess what? You need new clothes—and that means s-h-o-p-p-i-n-g! As you move into the tween and teenage groups, you may need braces—and you can choose some wacky color combination for your bands every time you go to the orthodontist. And one day you wake up and you've grown to a height that qualifies you for more rides at the amusement park. Yes, there are so many new things that fill your days with adventure!

And some of your new growth can be puzzling and even scary as your body changes and your responsibilities increase—like being in charge of your little brother or sister, helping with a new baby, or staying home alone until your parents get home from work.

Whatever is happening in your life, God's Word has help, answers, and sweet encouragement for you as you adventure through life with Jesus. So let's prepare to discover some radical truths about your S-E-L-F. Here we go!

Start each day with thanksgiving! Thank God each new morning for His love for you. Do you realize there is never a minute in your life when you are not special to God and loved by Him? He made you. He knows everything about you. And He loves you—no matter what.

How does this help a girl who's busy growing up, a girl who's in the process of becoming a girl after God's own heart? Well, it helps to realize that, no matter what's going on at home with your parents and brothers and sisters, or at school, God loves you. Or when you feel like you're not very special—to yourself or to anyone else—you can know that you are a treasure to God and greatly loved by Him. Or when the kids at school don't seem very friendly or nice, you can always bank on God's love for you. Soak in the fact of God's love as you look at these verses.

God so loved the world that he gave his one and only Son... (John 3:16). How great is God's love for His world and for you?

_____

_____

God has said, "Never will I leave you; never will I forsake you" (Hebrews 13:5). How strong and how long is God's love?

_____

_____

_____

njoy your life, yourself, your days. When I was a new Christian, I found Psalm 118:24. As I read it over and over and thought through the words, I made a decision. I decided that, before I even got out of bed each morning, I would begin each day with these words from Psalm 118:24:

> This is the day the LORD has made;
> let us rejoice and be glad in it.

You see, I had a bad habit. As soon as my alarm went off, I would start moaning and groaning and thinking, "Oh, no! Tell me it's not time to get up! I'm so tired! Someone give me a break!" But then I started remembering my decision to greet each new day with joy. So I would say these words in my heart or right out loud, no matter what was going on, no matter what I had to do that day: *This is the day the LORD has made; let us rejoice and be glad in it.*

I chose to start each day by remembering God and being glad. Even if I had a big test, I made God my first thought. Even if I was sick, rejoicing in God gave me a more joyful attitude. Even if I was going to the dentist (eek!), I reminded myself that because God was in charge of my day, I could be happy.

Don't get me wrong. I loved going to school. I mean, that's where my friends were. That's where my neat teachers were. That's where the action was. But there were always challenges. Like feeling I wasn't as pretty or cute or clever as some of the other girls. Like believing I was dumb when it came to math. Like wondering if anyone would play with me or hang out with me during lunch and recess.

Oh, there were lots of things I dreaded! Like being afraid I would give a wrong answer when the teacher called on me. Like taking the Friday spelling test. And there were things outside of school that I super dreaded...like my piano recitals. I loved music, and I loved practicing and playing the piano. But the recitals were pure 100 percent dread.

Do you know what helped me through the hard things in my days? Psalm 118:24! No matter what was ahead in my day, remembering that "this is the day the LORD has made" helped me to give the day to God and to rejoice, be glad, and enjoy it!

> *The fruit of the Spirit is...joy* (Galatians 5:22). What is a mark of a spirit-filled Christian who is walking by God's Spirit? Where does this quality come from?

> _____

> _____

Look inside your heart as much as you look in the mirror. Think about this "what if." What if there were a secret timer hidden inside your mirror that recorded how much time you spend looking at yourself? What do you think the total number of minutes—or hours!—would come to each day?

And here's a more important question: What do you see when you look at your reflection in your mirror? Most of us girls immediately see everything that's wrong with us—or what we *think* is wrong with us. Never mind our good features! Oh no, our eyes go straight to a nose we don't like, ears we think stick out, teeth we're sure will never straighten out. We seem to be made up of blemishes, hair that won't cooperate, and way too many freckles

It's impossible to escape mirrors. But here's one thing you can do about mirror-gazing: You can look in the mirror less often. Use it to make sure your appearance is neat and sends the message that you are a girl after God's own heart—innocent, modest, pure, and sweet. But once you know you look okay, move on to real life. Thank God for what you are becoming—a girl who is more concerned about her heart and character than her looks.

The LORD *does not look at the things man looks at. Man looks at the outward appearance, but the* LORD *looks at the heart* (1 Samuel 16:7). How is the Lord different from people? Where do people tend to focus their attention? Where does the Lord look instead?

_____

_____

_____

_____

_____

Focus on what God says is good about you. In God and through Christ, you are the object of His love. You are a trophy of His grace. You are, I hope, a member of the family of God. This is who you really are! No matter how you look or what abilities you have or don't have, you are precious to Him. As you look at the verse that follows, pay more attention to how God views you. Also be sure to notice the attitude He wants you to have about who you are.

I praise you because I am fearfully and wonderfully made; your works are wonderful... (Psalm 139:14). God never makes a mistake. What do you learn here about yourself?

_____

_____

_____

♥ HEART 2 HEART ♥

As I'm looking back over this chapter, my eyes are landing on words like "love," "joy," and "beauty." How positive is that? How wonderful is that? Yet why is it that we think of ourselves so negatively when God is constantly telling us how beautiful we are in His eyes? Why are we so hard on ourselves when God went to such great lengths—the death of His Son Jesus—to shout out and show His love for us? Why do we put ourselves down when God is expressing how pleased He is with us?

Sure, sometimes we make mistakes. We're unkind to someone, or we pay too much attention to what the "in" girls are wearing and want to dress like they do rather than God's way. And sometimes we get really moody and pouty.

But here's what's important to remember:

⚇ Remember you are fearfully and wonderfully made—exactly the way you are. God made you Himself, and He never makes a mistake!

⚇ Remember you can be joyful every second of every day—no matter what's happening to you—because God is with you.

⚇ Remember you are in a constant state of change as you grow year by year. Some of these changes are new, so make sure you talk these changes over with your mom.

⊚ Remember you are as special as a unique, one-of-a-kind snowflake, one of God's truly marvelous works!

Enjoy your journey with Jesus as you, like Him, grow "in wisdom and stature, and in favor with God and men" (Luke 2:52).

In this chapter we had some fun in God's Word learning about the importance of **S-E-L-F**. On this page, write out the point for each letter. (I'll get you started with "S.")

S tart each day with thanksgiving!

E _____

L _____

F _____

Now, write out one thing you liked, learned, or want to do about you and your self. Then enjoy the adventure!

_____

_____

_____

_____

_____

_____

_____

_____

_____

9

My Time

"What a day!" Emma muttered as she fell onto her bed. She was feeling absolutely dog-tired. She could hardly wait to turn out her light, lie down, and finally get some sleep. But just as Emma was about ready to drift off to sleep, another thought jarred her—she hadn't spent time with Jesus today. Her Sunday school teacher had asked the kids to find some minutes each day to read the Bible and pray. "Oh, well," Emma reasoned, "I just didn't have time today. And I'm too far gone now. I'll do it tomorrow."

Yes, Emma had done lots of activities. There was school all day. And after school there was practice for the school play. That was followed by a trip to the mall with her mom to pick out a birthday present for her brother. Her day had been so packed that it seemed like she didn't have any free time.

But as she thought about it, Emma had to admit she had wasted some time. She had put off doing her chores, daydreamed her way through her time before school, somehow managed to talk to all her friends on the phone, and dawdled through her homework, finishing just in time to go to bed. Even in what seemed like an impossibly busy day,

Emma could think of a lot of times when she could have done the most important thing—spend some time with Jesus.

FUN IN GOD'S WORD!

I think you and I can both identify with Emma's tiredness. And we can also identify with her realization that life is very busy. There just doesn't seem to be enough T-I-M-E in a day to do everything we need to. So let's take a look at how we *do* spend our time and how we *should* spend our time.

Time is a treasure. You would never throw away treasures like gold, silver, diamonds, and pearls, would you? As a girl after God's own heart, you shouldn't throw away your days and minutes either. Why? Because they too are riches and treasures!

You may not think a lot about the value of your time and what you spend it on. But God says it's wise to realize how precious time is. No one knows how long he or she will live, but we do know that we have *today*. And today is a treasure God has handed to you to spend and use wisely. Here's what God's Word says:

Teach us to number our days aright, that we may gain a heart of wisdom (Psalm 90:12). What is the result when we value each day and pay attention to how we spend our time?

_____

_____

It's important to "do it now." Do you have a bad habit of putting things off, especially if it's something you don't want to do? Your mom tells you to clean up your room or do your homework. But you tell yourself, "I'll do it later." Or you have a test coming up at school. Your teacher has warned the class every day for a week about this test. And still you haven't even started to study.

News flash! Guess what? Your messy room, your homework, and that test are not going to simply disappear into the misty realm of Neverland.

Do you know what putting things off is called? *Procrastination*. That's what we're doing—procrastinating—when we choose to put something off until later instead of doing it now. But God gives us a better way for getting things done. Read on!

> *I will hasten and not delay to obey your commands* (Psalm 119:60). What words in this verse speak to the importance of doing things now?

_____

_____

Make the most of your time. Emma thought there weren't enough hours in the day to do all the things she had to do and wanted to do. What does God's Word say about this?

> *There is a time for everything, and a season for every activity under heaven* (Eccesiastes 3:1). This verse says there

is a time for you to do all those things you want to do that are truly important!

Okay. Sometimes your days are jammed full of things you have to do. But here's another real-life scene. You're at home...and it seems like there is absolutely nothing to do! No one's around to play with. You've done your schoolwork and all your chores. In fact, you've done about everything you can *think* of doing! So out of your mouth comes a big sigh and those dreadful words—"I'm bored!"

Oh dear! Do you want to know the secret to never being bored again? Here it is. Make a list of "5 Things I Want to Do." The things on your list can include goals or dreams, hobbies, a series of books you'd like to read, something you'd love to know about or learn to do.

Do you realize how truly exciting some free time could be? It gives you the opportunity to work on writing a book, complete with your own illustrations. You can also write to a missionary or a pen pal. You can pull out your craft box and make something for someone special. You can draw a comic book story. You can design and make jewelry. You can read through the Little House on the Prairie books from the library, or the Anne of Green Gables series. You can enjoy time with your doll collection, and sew clothes for the dolls. You can even work on a personal Bible study that's just for you.

There are loads of things you can learn to do. You can use your down time to learn how to do neat things with your hair, how to knit or make beaded jewelry. If you have a camera, you can spend this time taking pictures of flowers, insects, and cool scenes. You can even read a library book on photography.

I know your parents determine how a great deal of your time is spent. But you probably still have a lot of free time every day—time when you can choose what you do. It's easy to think about turning on the TV and vegging out (like Emma did). It's easy to fill your free time playing a game on the computer or a handheld game player. But once you make your list, you'll find there are far more exciting ways to spend your time. You'll never again say, "I'm bored!"

As we've been learning, time is a treasure. And, like our verse said, we are to value each day and pay attention to how we spend our time. I've put five lines here so you can get started on your list of...

5 THINGS I WANT TO DO

1. _____

2. _____

3. _____

4. _____

5. _____

Evaluate your priorities. A priority is something that's more important than other things. There are many ways you can use your time. Now, the question is, how can you begin to choose the *best* options over options that are not the best?

Many of your activities—like school—have been decided for you by others. Others, like sports, music lessons, and church activities, have been established for you by your parents. Plus you have your chores at home. These priorities are "set in stone." So how does God want you to approach these established priorities?

> *Whatever you do, whether in word or deed, do it all in the name of the Lord Jesus* (Colossians 3:17). How are you to do everything, including taking care of your important tasks?

_____

_____

_____

If you don't do some planning (as Emma discovered!), time with Jesus can get crowded out of your life. Jesus does not want you to neglect school, family, or other important activities. But, just as you set aside time to go to school or practice a musical instrument, you need to plan time to meet with God. You need to pick a time when you will read His Word and pray. Spending time with Jesus is the most important priority you have every day. Look at these great verses and circle the word "seek" in each verse:

Seek first his kingdom and his righteousness (Matthew 6:33).

Blessed [happy] are they who keep his statutes and seek him with all their heart (Psalm 119:2).

I seek you with all my heart (Psalm 119:10).

O God, you are my God, earnestly I seek you (Psalm 63:1).

♥ HEART 2 HEART ♥

I hope you are beginning to realize how important your time is, especially when it comes to time with Jesus. You make Jesus a priority when you make a commitment to spend time with Him. Would you fail to show up for a meeting with a teacher? Would you skip a friend's birthday party? I don't think so! So why would you not want to make time for Jesus, the most important person in the world?

When you spend time with Jesus, great things happen! He makes your days more exciting. He gives you a happy heart. He helps you do your best and do it in a way that honors Him. He shows you how to be more kind and helpful to others. And He does His amazing work of transforming you into what you really want to be—a girl after His own heart! Then, when you put your head on your pillow at night, instead of feeling bad (like Emma did), you can thank Jesus for a wonderful day!

In this chapter we had some fun in God's Word learning about the importance of **T-I-M-E**. On this page, write out the point for each letter. (I'll get you started with "T.")

Time is a treasure.

I _____

M_____

E _____

Now, write out one thing you liked, learned, or want to do about how you spend your time. Then enjoy the adventure!

_____

_____

_____

_____

_____

_____

_____

_____

10

My Adventure with Jesus

Wow, what a trip! I can't believe all the things we've talked about on our journey together with Jesus. I truly hope you've enjoyed our adventure. I know I have!

As we've traveled along, we've seen Emma struggle with daily life at home, school, church, and with friends. (Could you relate?) We've looked at some of the key areas of a tween girl's life. We've also discussed what it means to be a girl after God's own heart—a girl who wants to know God and do His will.

Before we go our separate ways, here are a few key things to remember about Jesus and your heart and life. I'm sure you're not surprised that brings up another acrostic! Actually, it's a sentence. (And, of course, it spells J-E-S-U-S.)

Jesus, the Son of God,

Entered this world as a baby, and

Sacrificed Himself for sinners to

Unite them with the Father by

Securing eternal life for all who believe in Him.

Did you notice that throughout this book we've talked about Jesus and about being a Christian? Maybe you've been asking, "What does it mean to be a Christian? Am I a Christian? How can I become a Christian?"

By now you are probably not surprised to know that the Bible tells us how to have a personal relationship with Jesus. Here are a few verses, often called "The Romans Road." That's because every verse on this "road" is from the book of Romans in the New Testament of the Bible.

THE ROMANS ROAD

Romans 3:23 tells you about your sinful condition—*All have sinned and fall short of the glory of God.*

Romans 6:23 shows you the result of your sinful condition and reveals the gift God offers to you instead—*The wages of sin is death, but the gift of God is eternal life in Christ Jesus our Lord.*

Romans 5:8 points out God's grace and love for you and Christ's solution to your sinful condition—*God demonstrates his own love for us in this: While we were still sinners, Christ died for us.*

Romans 10:9-10 reveals some steps to take to become a Christian—*If you confess with your mouth, "Jesus is Lord," and believe in your heart that God raised him from the dead, you will be saved.*

I meet girls—and women—all the time who are not sure if they are a Christian or not. They want to be a Christian, but don't know how.

The way to become a Christian is to receive Jesus Christ as your personal Savior. If being a Christian and becoming a child of God is the desire of your heart, you can pray a sincere prayer from your heart like this one:

A PRAYER TO PRAY

God, I want to be Your child, a true girl after Your heart—a girl who lives her life in You, and through You, and for You, not for myself. I admit that I am a sinner and often fail to do what You say is right. I receive Your Son, Jesus Christ, into my needy heart. I thank You that He died on the cross for my sins. Thank You for giving me Your grace and Your strength so that I can follow You with all my heart. Amen.

HEART 2 HEART

As you finish this book and come to the end of this adventure with Jesus, guess what? It's not the end! That's because you will continue to walk with Jesus all through life. You'll continue your journey with Jesus and grow more and more as the years pass. For instance:

- You're going to grow in love—love for Jesus, love for your family, and love for others.

- You're going to grow in the knowledge of God's Word as you read your Bible, go to church, and surround yourself with friends who love Jesus, too.

- You're going to grow in wisdom so you don't make too many mistakes. You'll learn what's right and what's wrong. And you'll learn to make wise choices as you read your Bible and talk with your parents and other Christians.

- You'll grow in God's grace as you hit roadblocks or speed bumps along the way and experience trials. But praise God, His grace is sufficient to see you through and teach you how to handle your problems.

- You'll grow in joy as you fall more and more in love with Jesus and walk closely with Him. The joy of the Lord will strengthen you for every challenge. And you'll know real joy as God rewards you for every victory, accomplishment, and achievement you experience by His grace.

God has great plans for you. Finishing this book is just one step toward discovering His plan. So congratulations on completing this part of the journey to becoming a girl after God's own heart! Keep on keeping on. Your adventure has only just begun!

Notes

1. Missionary Jim Elliot wrote this in his personal journal. Jim was one of five missionaries who were killed by jungle natives more than 50 years ago in Ecuador. Jim was the husband of Christian author Elisabeth Elliot.

2. Roy B. Zuck, *The Speaker's Quote Book* (Grand Rapids, MI: Kregel, 1997), p. 159.

3. Adapted from "A Grandmother's Prayer," from The Grandmother's Bible (Grand Rapids, MI: Zondervan, 2008), p. 1622.

MY NOTES

Books by Elizabeth George for Teen Girls

A Young Woman After God's Own Heart

What does it mean to include God's heart in your everyday life? It means understanding and following His perfect plan for your friendships, your faith, your family relationships, and your future. Learn how to grow close to God, enjoy meaningful relationships, make wise choices, become spiritually strong, build a better future, and fulfill the desires of your heart.

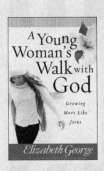

A Young Woman's Walk with God

Love, joy, peace, patience, kindness, goodness, faithfulness, gentleness, and self-control are qualities Jesus possessed—and He wants you to have them too! Elizabeth George takes you step by step through the fruit of the Spirit to help you get the most out of your life.

A Young Woman's Call to Prayer

God has given you an amazing gift—
the ability to talk with Him every day!
Through prayer, you can share with God
your joys and triumphs, hurts and fears,
wants and needs. He cares about every
detail of your life. God is your forever
friend, and He's always ready to talk
with you!

A Young Woman's Guide to Making Right Choices

When it comes to making decisions, how
can you make sure you are making the
right choices, the best choices? Do you
desire to please God in the way you pick
your friends, spend your time, and treat
your family? You'll find useful check-
points for helping you understand God's
wisdom and live it out.

A Young Woman After God's Own Heart— A Devotional

God wants to encourage you each and every day! He has things to say to you that can change your day, take away your worries, and give you hope. In His amazing love, He cares about all the details of your life. In this pocket-sized devotional, you'll learn how to take your problems to God, let go of your worries, live your faith, find a real friend in Jesus, and grow in true beauty and confidence.